For Sandra —

C000121343

Volum
Book of
LIVED

Penny Authors

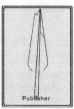

Publisher

MA PUBLISHER

CONTENTS

Introduction

Welcome to the 7th accomplishment of the Penny Authors' Anthology. The previous anthologies have been a success and as a result we have attracted new poets in this edition. This volume sees us accomplishing some mile stones, we have organically reached 52 poets including artists, out of which we have 24 female and 28 male; so we have a healthy balanced representation of both gender and diversity.

The experiences that are captured in the anthology are colourful and the times that they've happened give it the flavour. PA wants to bring to the world, the world within and show the abundances to our lives. We all ride "the ride of life" from different points but all travel to the heart, the centre of what life is.

In this book you will feel and experience journeys that will take you in and out, emotionally, mentally and spiritually. You can let yourself get on a ride that will become a merry-go-round, then may turn into a roller coaster ride, it will take you through life of all ages and some; be it familiar experiences and occurrences or to some out of this world or weird and something wonderful.

This is the seventh instalment of the "book of lived," that lets you live life outside of yours. If you would like to get involved then email pennyauthors@yahoo.co.uk.

We at Penny Authors like to recognise, remind and remember all the Penny Authors that have taken part, past always and present; and you can find the full list in the back of the book. The following list is to introduce the newcomers who are featured in this volume. They bring with them refreshing and unique life they've lived for us to read, enjoy and experience; each to their own take. The newcomers are:

1. Stuart Cooper
2. Mustak Mostafa
3. Ferdous Rahman
4. Ossian Hughes
5. Steve Willoughby
6. Ayesha Chowdhury
7. Samuil Fox
8. Abu Maryam Gous
9. Abul Hussain
10. Libby Pentreath
11. Paul Phillips
12. Adrian Smith (Artist)

So see you on the other side email us on pennyauthors@yahoo.co.uk.
Finally, we hope you will enjoy reading the Book of Lived.

Impossible Not To Love
by Stuart Cooper

Every now and then in life.
Someone comes along.
The type of person for whom you could.
Compose a special song.
They just have something about them.
But they don't seek attention.
When it comes to personality traits.
There are far too many to mention.
Well I've come across such a person.
Since I've been in Powys Ward.
And whenever she's around you.
It's impossible to be bored.
I've tried my best to hate her.
But it's impossible to do.
You just can't help but crack up.
If she simply looks at you.
She's full of fun and mischief.
And Shauna is her name.
I swear to you I've never met.
Anyone quite the same.
So how can I describe her.
Well, she's an Angel from above.
With more than a hint of devilment.
And impossible not to love.

Trying Hard To Fail
by Stuart Cooper

Not a bad bone in his body.
No harm was ever meant.
Being loving, kind, friendly and true.
On this he was hell bent.
He lived his life on eggshells.
Through fear of being offensive.
But he'd walk where others are not tread.
When it came to being defensive.
Despite his respect and morals.
No matter how hard he tried.
He'd ultimately upset someone.
Then he'd die a bit inside.
Nothing but devastation.
The feeling that would remain.
Thank god this freak can barely face.
Seeing the world again.
Being nice gets him nowhere.
Compliments just backfire.
He may as well just count down time.
'Til he's upon the funeral pyre.
Darkness, the route to enlightenment.
Or at least that's what they say.
But I bet if you wore his shoes.
You seriously m wouldn't last a day.

Always The Same Outcome
by Stuart Cooper

No matter just how hard he tried.
He'd never quite fit in.
It's a if being 'one of them'.
Had become a cardinal sin.
With the very best of intentions.
Whilst always seeking peace.
He'd always know within himself.
Whatever's good will cease.
In the past, within his hands.
The world was his to hold.
But ke knew, no matter how hard he tried.
His deck of cards would fold.
He'd be jilted by a loved one.
Or lose his state of employment.
He'd lose everything that gave him.
A sense of purpose or enjoyment.
All of a sudden the world went dark.
No brightness to explore.
This seems how it's going to be.
For now and evermore.
So he'd just accept the bad things.
The trouble, shit and strife.
Because no matter how hard he tried.
He'd always fail at life.

Hello Darkness My Old Friend
by Stuart Cooper

It's just an inevitability.
When life creeps up on you.
Best intentions met with disdain.
Is just what life will do.
You try to outrun darkness.
Such a difficult task.
Sprinting hard for just a glimpse of light.
Is that too much to ask?
Even when surrounded by angels.
Hell knocks at my door.
I try to do right, it always goes wrong.
I think, 'what am I living for?
Living in a world of violent rage.
But it's one that I can recognise.
Because I'm one of many people.
That's never seen his father's eyes.
So, yes I dwell in hell.
But it's a hell that I can grip.
I tried to grip my family.
But as usual I slipped.
Could I escape from the pain.
Trapped in this existence mundane.
Just get a line of cyanide set.
And then I've got a name.
So will people see the writing.
Sprayed angrily on life's wall?
As I'm certain nobody out there.
Can catch me when I fall.

The Greatest Gift Of All
by Stuart Cooper

Gifts can come in many forms.
Most are gratefully received.
You watch with dread as they open yours.
And when they like it, you're relieved.
But there's one gift that trumps them all.
It doesn't come under a tree.
You'll want to keep it your whole life.
It could come to you, as it has to me.
It's the gift that keeps on giving.
Yet it takes a fair bit, too.
It's a gift that's sent to test us.
But bring out the best in you.
You'll treasure it immediately.
You'll be grateful this gift is yours.
And the longer that you have it.
You'll do nothing but open doors.
I'm speaking metaphorically.
Not in the literal sense.
To look after this gift properly.
Will make you feel immense.
So do not take it lightly.
As it's simply just too good.
To be truly blessed is to receive.
The gift of parenthood.

Acceptance And Resignation
by Stuart Cooper

When tragedy creeps upon you.
In your heart, that's nothing new.
You just can't help but ponder.
If it's simply down to you.
Because it happens so much.
In a world that does revolve.
Bad things always come around.
Is this a problem I can solve?
It's one thing after another.
Blow after crushing blow.
You exchange punches, but in the end.
You know which way it will go.
You try to be a good person.
Your treat others with respect.
Yet you fail at being a nice guy.
But what did you expect?
It isn't a coincidence.
That bad luck follows you around.
It kicks you, hits you, beats you.
And stomps you into the ground.
So it's finally time for acceptance.
The last right thing to do.
The fault and reason for all bad stuff.
Is solely down to you!

The End Will Come, It's Just How!
by Stuart Cooper

The sun comes up, the world spins around.
On this you can depend.
They're the only guarantees in life.
Except for taxes and meeting life's end.
You can't depend on people.
Who can't depend on themself.
You're destined for the scrapheap.
After teetering on life's shelf.
You've taken all that's thrown at you.
Your loved ones are all gone.
You reach and reach for positives.
But realise there's none.
The roads you drive are twisty.
Not as twisted as your soul.
Only you could take a penalty.
That results in an own goal.
Other folk look down on you.
Is that true, or what you think?
It's ultimately where you've placed yourself.
As down that hole you sink.
Let life become your teacher.
As in the end it's death that wins.
The invisible man in the sky cars not.
If you've lived life with no sins.

Dancing With The Wind
by Ferdous Rahman

What a wonderful feeling
Dancing with the wind
helping me to ignore
unjust surroundings.

I can make it happen
While I am dancing
I will change the world
The way I want in our way
The way for all of us.

Global Warning
by Ferdous Rahman

What is happening
Does anyone know?
Are we going to wrap
In a green house?
Some say ice caps are melting
Some blame it on Global Warming.

Mother Nature knows best
Which one to protect
And which one to waste
The rule is the survival
For the fittest.

Emitting carbon dioxide
Blocking the Sun
All alarming news
We become stunned
How are we going to survive?
How are we going to thrive?

The nature provides
More than we deserve
Chlorophyll and stress
We should increase
Use less more we conserve.
27.05.2007

Dragon-Slayer
by Ferdous Rahman

Magic or Myth!
Which do you believe?
It happened in the past
An angelic Saint with a red cross

Dragons protect us in the East
In the West it's a wicked Beast
Oh St. George you made
The impossible the reality
Rescued people from eternity.
19.04.2007

Green Fingers
by Ferdous Rahman

My husband wanted
To be useful in the garden

I said OK,
Why don't you weed?

He weeded the garden
Removed all the flowering plants;

Keeping all the weeds.
I was upset.

But I said Why don't you plant
Onions and marigold seeds?

Weeks passed, no sign of shoots.
Everything was planted upside down.

I will buy you more plants, he said
Don't worry! Which made me angry.

Plants take time to grow
Then the winter will follow.

Even though it was late
I showed him how to grow pumpkins.

He became the best
Pumpkin grower in the borough.

His Pumpkins died too soon.
He moved on to trees.

Now all round the garden
We have his pear trees, his apple trees,

Grapes and crab-apples
Cherries and more ....

All his trees remain.
He disappeared.

Equality

by Ferdous Rahman

Women can vote but not equal
They do more work then, men.
They managed home, business and office.
Yet they are neglected and become invisible.
No women want sympathy but opportunity.
At work, family, relationship, seems unreachable.
Same work women do, pay scale is different.
All accumulated work they do.
Compare with man's job is it equal too?
Of course not!

Women gives birth to male child,
Until they are full grown.
Remain under mother's care and love.
What goes wrong then?
Men do love and care for their mother,
What happens to wife and girlfriends and others?
They are also someone's mother too.

Domestic violence and physical and mental
Abuse going strong in disguise.
Who controls these? Of course it's men's job.
But why?
Why these discriminations?
Why do they do?
Need proper investigation.
What we preach we should practice.
Until all these inequalities, injustices end.
Please do something men!

Black Lives Matters
by Ferdous Rahman

Since black lives matters appeared on surface
I felt better at last
What was unjust no one could see.
It was wrong inequality, only pointing towards,
Who's colour of skin not white.
They were totally blind.
What a cruel way to treat!
Could you accept business as slaves merchant?
Their statues were displayed in public places in disguise.
White supremacy so powerful, Legal history,
Would not do justice for weak and voiceless.
Better things are happening and visible now.

Donald Trump was defused like gas balloon.
Like to see more positive changes all around
Bring back the justice, what was our right
Dark skin is not a crime!
It is a process of evolution.
We have to be vigilant forever,
Without any fail and fatigue, to time to relax.
Otherwise it will be same again.
Do not let it go hold the rein.
Forever until equality remain.

Beaver And The Litter Bug.
by Steve Willoughby

The Beaver with a tail flat like a paddle , his coat was water poof like a wet suit. The Beaver swam slowly and gently, gliding down the steam, looking for bits and bobs to build his home; with his family. Safe and secure .

Now it is the time of year, when life become hard. Plastic here old shopping carts there in the pound ,litter bugs everywhere . Bins overflowing ,even where the posters say ;please take your rubbish home with you.

The litter bugs says never mind the fish, beavers and the other animals ,they will not know it was us that left the pots and pans . The animals don't understand anything .

The Beavers by this time, they were sick to their teeth of the litter bugs ,and decided to move on but where? There sweet smelling home with fresh clear water was gone , it had been transformed into a smelly ,stinky and black like tar.

Fishes looking like a blanket covering the whole pond . has life gone for good? The Beavers thought to themselves , how far do we need to go ,to get fresh air and clear water full of life .

Litter bugs litter bugs what have you done .where has the clear water gone, and all the wild animals gone .

Will life ever return? Where the flowers use to brighten up the land by the pond . And the air was full of aroma , and the fishes ,frog ,beavers lived like friends happy full of smile on their faces as they went along life way.

All of the sudden the litter bugs had a light bulb moment a flash of light. yes yes yes , I know what to do . what said the other litter bugs ,do tell us don't keep us in dark any longer or I will wet myself Come on come on. With a deep breath we could clean up our mess.

when all the clean up was done , and the water was clear as a window, shining in the sun . Life started to return , but we will have to wait until next year, to find out what has happened to the Beaver family.

Human Fallacy
by Mustak A. Mustafa

Long as the sun sets and rises
Starry nights will bring surprises
Rebellious curtains of the skies
Will give rise to shiny nights
Bringing back memories
Awakening the glories
Reborn and revised poetry in motion
No fear has faith in creation
Time has bought doubt they will laugh
Those who know more will further guff
The sun merely hangs in motion they will rebuff
Like a grain in the distance
Laugh they will at an instance
Those who know
But still others follow
Standing beneath the starlit sky
The mind can fly by
Stars do dance and mingle
As opposed to alone and single
Soon enough they disappear
The heart longs for them to appear
The mind seeks to join the stars
And to the kingdom of theirs
Where peace may prevail
Wonder if my dreams will be real.

Peace
by Mustak A. Mustafa

What is this pain that has possessed me
What is it that burns I cannot see
What be this ache that pains
What be this burn that reigns
I feel the end is nigh
Spreading through my soul high
I am separated
I feel alone and isolated
I can bear this pain no more
Loneliness I detest for sure
Restlessness in abundance
Peace seems distant
I long to relieve this strife
I want peace I want life
I want love
Peace to have
Feed me not to this fierce throng
I cannot tolerate this I do not feel strong
I want love
Peace to have

Lovers Abode
by Mustak A. Mustafa

Your smile
Makes me irrational

Your twinkling eyes
Makes my heart rise

Your tender smile
Plays music for miles

When the time comes round
Melody will sound

Bride's arrival will sign
You're new home at mine

Your angst will rapture
Coz' married life will capture

Your heart load
As you enter your lovers abode

Awaiting
by Mustak A. Mustafa

The force of the waters erodes the shores
The river flows careless ignoring the moors
Storm wrecks havoc on passers by
Birds are clueless flying high
Nests lie empty smashed in ruins
Hovering, homeless
Fly off helpless
Lost and forlorn weeping alone
None can put right
Nature evades their plight
How they long to find sanctuary
From their pain this misery
Memories flood in, passing by
Fragrant flowers scents so high
When will it come again?
I wait in vain
For our meeting

Illusion
by Mustak A. Mustofa

One mid afternoon
Along the streets of London
Amongst the crowd
Wondering around

Startled as I saw you
Momentarily found you
It is you, you have come
By my side as I am

Rushed forward
Doubts removed
I realised
Its not you, its my eyes

Someone else
Momentarily taken your place
In my eyes
I realised

I Have Nothing To Tell You

by Sandra Green

I have nothing to tell you
No deeds to recount
No witty rapport to
Impress with account.
I cannot recall a task or a thought
That's worth repetition
Though maybe I ought
To mention that I,
With my doddering stance
Did manage today,
An impetuous dance.
I threw off dull care
With a nonchalant shrug
Unhooked the curtain
With one mighty tug
Then wrapped it around me
In Romanesque style,
As I swung to the left
And then, in a while
I swung to the right
Until I caught sight
Of me in the mirror
And ,oh what a fright!

I'm Looking For A Gentleman
by Sandra Green

I'm looking for a gentleman
Of six foot two or more.
He needn't be a millionaire
But, then again, not poor.
I'd like him to be handsome
And supple, if not spry,
And I'd like him to be able
To tackle DIY.
I will not do his washing,
Cook his meals or clean his loo.
I draw the line at personal care
And fornication too.
I'll let him buy me dinner
Hold my hand and drive me home
But I need to make this very clear
I ALWAYS SLEEP ALONE!

I'm fond of cats and music
And poetry and prose
I'm a pacifist, a vegan
And a hippie to my toes.
My hips are wide, my hair is long
And often needs a comb.
I'm generous with my worldly goods
BUT MY BODY IS MY OWN.
So if you voted labour
And love your dear old mum.
If all you want is friendship
When all is said and done,
I may be what you're looking for
To while away the time
Till you go home to your house
AND I GO HOME TO MINE!

What Does Love Feel Like?
by Sandra Green

What does love feel like?

Love feels like a finger popping,
heart thumping,
belly churning explosion of joy.

It's a hand clenching,
eye watering roller coaster ride of whooping,
wailing and whimpering that,
if you're lucky, lasts a lifetime.

It's a key in the door grin,
a goodnight hug,
a raging roaring passion and a gentle,
soothing stroke.

Love is everything.
It gets you up in the morning,
carries you through the day and gives you peace at night.

Love feels like belonging,
like snuggling down in a safe harbour.

It is not fleeting,
is not some airborne thing that vanishes on the breeze.

Love survives dull days and fitful nights,
mundane chores and sharp words.

Love is when you look towards me and I catch your eye.
Love is the beat that my heart misses.

Child of Love
by Ossian Hughes

Child of Love
Fawns
After a dawn yawn
Seed sown under gown
Blown down
A feathered hole

Dove In Red Silk
by Ossian Hughes

Dove In Red Silk
Flew on injured wing
To fall on green
Die unseen
But was the dove really a pigeon

When Things Go All Wrong
by Samiul Fox

U feel as though
everything's gone.
The life you are
walking is spiralling
down.

It's hard not to frown.

When debts are high
income is low.

Stress is on its peak
days passing by so slow.

U feel like doing nothing.

Stress level getting high.
u lose your smile
and gain a sigh.

Don't be afraid you
are not alone

Don't be a quitter
it's not all gone.

moral of my poem..

never give up hope and
don't be afraid to
talk to someone about your stress.

Hanbury And Hobsons 1983- 1998
by Samiul Fox

Raised by Hobsons N Hanbury.
Our little area, decent, humble and friendly.
Ordinary boys, having fun.
Not chasing Burberry.
Isolated from the rest.
It was our cosy nest.
It was our boroughs mirage.
Had our little camps by the garage.
Respected our guest.
Treated them the best.
Never into bling.
Respected our elders.
Looked at our father's as king.
Let's get to the fun part.
Come summer,
every kids out.
No one's a loner.
Making catapults, water fighting,
ain't going home till the parents are shouting.
Football, Chinese, knockout, it.
Packing it in till the street lamps lit.
Hopscotch, stickers , wall game..
kids don't play this no more,
Shame..
we were a quite bunch,
never chased Gangsta fame.
this place was a gem.
Hanbury and Hobson was the name.
memories 4 ever..
life would never be the same.

Brick Lane
by Samiul Fox

Our little community
Bangla Town is its adopted name
has its own fame
titled UK's curry lane
also has the famous dog market
selling fruits, bikes, rags and carpet
You name it, has the lot
Brick Lane our gem
our own golden pot
it raised 2 generation
old skool had it tough
dealing with the racial discrimination
all because they wanted Brick Lane
evolving into a Bengali nation.
Never forget your roots.
Respect to our elders
we can never fill their boots.

CUZ
by Samiul Fox

You are afraid of me coz I am brown.
The media has turned my nation into a evil clown...

Left right centre we are getting killed...
While your offspring's are flourishing n getting skilled...
When I step into bus number 25 with a back pack...
I can see your face saying 'gulp' step back.
U have every reason to, my religion has been hijacked.

Extremists and suicide bombers using us.
They don't care about the ordinary people facing the back lash.

Media painting us all with the same brush and
constantly labelling all of us as terrorists is a bit harsh.

Hate is being spread via the net and brains are being washed.

The pawns are fighting while the kings and queens are selling arms,
profiting and getting their minerals and cheques cashed.

The world needs a saviour fast, the world needs peace,
a peace that would last.

Fair law for all, equal and just.
ending all the wars is a must.

Peace be upon you, peace to the world.
stay blessed and strong, cuz.
PS .....
life's a test, those who pray,
respect others and help the needy,
you are amongst the best.

Welcome to Hunton

by Samiul Fox

This is a story of
A small group of boys
from East London.
(Part of crew BLM).

Our destiny began from a school named
Thomas Buxton.
Our hang about was
by MacGlashon.
Most of us puffed our
first ciggy by that
old spooky lookin mansion
twos, save, butt...
Hunton was the heart.
Will always reminisce
those golden days
we had...

Don't get me wrong,
we weren't bad.
Streets of East London, this
upbringing was a norm.
but A total different
game at our home.
most would get smack
for doin anything wrong.
alright,
cut me the slack
enough of that,
it's getting long.
Back to Hunton.
one for all and
all for one,
this was us.
we had passion.
come juvenile scene,
we were up there,

cont.

reppin it with fashion.
slick, smart, hair style was curtain.
French crop, step and
all sorts of pattern.
cool as platinum.

The boys of Hunton.
prepared and clued on.
We were from all corners
Roman, Shoreditch and Bethnal.
Them good old days gone.
Sick memories of our own.
Some memoir unable to share.
Too hardcore,
your eyes won't be able to bare.

BLESS THE YOUNG AND OLD OF HUNTON.
STAY SAFE AND TAKE CARE ❤

Never Felt Like This Before
by Ayesha Chowdhury

Love yourself, love others.
A big smile, satisfaction and pleasure
you can get everything by loving unconditionally.

Why should that matter if anyone loves you or not,
as long as you have the capacity to love, to give,
- you could discover a planet that is so beautiful.

I never knew until I was told that I could drain all the pain,
with soothing touch of my eyes, with a few loving words...
I didn't realised that I could do this with my selfless love,
miraculous Midas touch.

When you are proud to have someone in your life,
When you expect nothing,
but just to give everything.

When your love makes someone speak their heart,
When you give them strength,
When you make their life worthwhile.

When you make them fight their negativity,
When you can take all their tears, and make them smile;
you become number one lover of the world, the greatest.

You then experience the indescribable pleasure,
you experience the feeling that you never felt like this before.
you experience love, the magic.

Naive - I Don't Understand
by Ayesha Chowdhury

I am not saying that I was craving for food.
But I found myself beside the table,
full of delicious dishes, a wide variety of food,
the fragrance was just heavenly.
If I can't wait for an invitation,
How could that be degraded?
I don't understand.

Any time,
I listen to the music of rain,
I just cannot keep myself indoor.
I continue to walk in the rain,
I get so much pleasure that cannot be described,
I get temperature soon after.
How is that my fault?
I don't understand.

When I see a green tree with or without red and pink flowers,
any time I hear a bird singing,
when I am passing by a beautiful canal,
I cannot resist myself from taking a selfie!
How could that be an addiction?
I don't understand.

I am not saying that I had a thirst for love.
However, If I am constantly reminded how beautiful,
creative, kind and caring I am.
If I see a new me in the mirror,
If I start loving me more than anything else,
If I start singing, dancing, and laughing loud.
Why should I be called crazy?
I don't understand.

I am so naive,
nothing I can understand.
However, I know I am happy
and nothing more I need to understand.

International Women's Day –
by Ayesha Chowdhury

I am calling you naive,
I am saying that you don't deserve to be independent or equal!
If you have the guts to challenge me,
I will apologise, if you don't, it makes me right.

You don't get me do you?

Your male counterpart thinks he is the best,
he accepts all the challenges,
and he thinks he is stronger than you.

You are a woman,
you are taught to accept what he says in your heart and brain,
you are the loser before you even enter the fight.

Well you might be different,
you may not believe what he says.
However, since you are a peace loving woman,
you think about the future consequences,
so you decided to remain quiet for the sake of peace
and you are the loser yet again.

You are never weak, until you cry for pity.
You are always equal, until you expect sympathy,
until you expect a paid holiday,
until you expect someone else to do it for you.

My dear sisters,
you need to believe in yourself you need to empower yourself,
you need to do what is right for you,
you need to claim your independency and equality,
you need to tell others what you like and dislike,
you have to fight for every single right.

Time To Change
by Ayesha Chowdhury

Time and thoughts are changing,
people have also changed.
The woman were once oppressed,
Men are experiencing that bitterness today.

We used to get lots of stories in the past about
abused daughter in laws.
I have done so many conflict solutions.

However, today that story has changed.
Mother-in-laws are spending night in Police Station
and not only that sometimes they are victims too.

Time and thoughts are changing, people have also changed.
I wish to see no one oppressed by their fellow human being.
I wish to see people understand their rights as well as
responsibilities and duty.

Men and women, all are human.
For everyone's happiness,
you have to make yourself happy.

Men and women must work together as a good citizen.
This is the only way you can build a beautiful world and live in a
peaceful city.
Looking forward to a great day and an amazing planet to live.

[05/02/2021]

Overpriced Love
by Ayesha Chowdhury

From jewellery to shoes,
bags, or cars.
Thoughts of shopping makes me worried.
Prices are increasing on everything.

However,
whatever you want to get,
it's not only overpriced but overcrowded too.

There is one thing though,
the price of which is constantly decreasing;
it's called 'Love',

We are no more human,
constantly acting like machines.
At this century do we still have time for unreal-love?

Yet on this evil business of love,
you still have to push the crowd to find love.
It is also very crowded.

Friends,
not love,
try to be happy with commitment.

Best wishes.

So This Is Us
by Chris York

The world moves much too fast
It's a wonder how life can last
Upon this small
Colourful ball
Where people think they know it all.
It's not for me to reason why
But tell me something what's the sky
Would you say that we were born
To fight, to hate and to scorn
No you couldn't admit all this
and make your life a perfect miss
Or is it that we are too proud
To shout the truth right out loud.
So tell me why we make a joke
About the poor and unfortunate folk.
Stop
And think for a while
And see you neighbours start to smile
It would be a special place
To see happiness on everyone's face
So stop your grabbing
And start giving
And praise the Lord we are still
Living.

A poem written in a sock factory's toilet on the back of a time and motion
sheet whilst on a break in 1969 at the age of 16 by Chris York.

The News
by Chris York

When the news came
We were devastated
As if blinded by onions
For it was father
Yes it was he
Who had cancelled
THE BEANO.

Injustice
by Chris York

I was so depressed
So I confessed
To the crime I had committed
They said don't worry
You're in no hurry
Your stay has been admitted

Behind the wall
You've lost it all
Freedom you have not
But that's ok
You're on your way
To hell and it's bloody hot

In that one cell
Where you can yell
And yet no one will ever hear
You can shout and scream
And hide in a dream
Until the hour when they'll appear

Yes they'll lead you straight
To the gallows gate
Where you'll stand
And watch your last sun
But what the heck
A noose round my neck
For the crime that I have done.

Pig Ignorant
by Chris York

(This somebody, everyone knows)

Bloated is hi stomach
Empty is his mind
Some people say
It's food for thought
But he's not that kind

An Equation.
by Chris York

Astound yourself by laughing at injustice
Or
the inequality of mankind
Open wide the mouth of plenty
And fill it with the piety of a pig
How many beans make five
Swallowed the starving adjudicator
Whilst counting all the shrapnel
Of two world wars.

Disaster
by Chris York

The grass was green
The skies were blue
The air's polluted
And so are you.

Process
by Abu Maryam Gous

Automation as a process
to the limitation
of a population

Formalisation
of the degradation of a nation

Artificial
not real intelligence
replacing the division of labour
Process of erosion in human corrosion

Life
by Abu Maryam Gous

A new lease of life....
Do we have a freehold on life...?
To own it outright....
Is there an inheritance on it,
who is there to inherit it...?
Bargaining with life....

XYZ
by Abu Maryam Gous

Fearless on the path to success
and the Ambition to be....x, y and zee.

When there's only one place to be...
The destination is set,
so where else will you be....

Contentment at the realisation
 of the world that be.....

Calmness on the sea
The path that lead to where peace be within me.....

Dress to Impress
by Abu Maryam Gous

Dressed to impress nowhere to go
yet you address....
The shoe fits like a glove....
yet they say you're too big for your boots....
Kicked to the curb you defend your perspective....
driven by an illusion yet you succumb to their perception.....
Critical of their position you desire a solution.....
Ultimate sacrifice, you give up your ambition.....
That fat lady that never sings, it ain't over till it's over.....
Down trodden yet not down under.....6ft still to go.....
Don't let them hold you back....it's not a sequel.....
Its just the shadow..... till it's there no more
We live and learn, then learn a bit more....
learn till we can't learn no more

Final
by Abu Maryam Gous

Whose country?
Yours, mine?
Ours?

What is the duration of our occupation
An earth deserving ovation
The nomadic shifting in motion
The limbs final destination

What is there?
look carefully, My G.

We occupy a particular space at any given time
as though drifting and hovering until our time comes to an end.
That very same space, will be occupied by another.
The shift in our residency, is like that of the nomads
moving from space to space.
Never remaining in the same place forever.....

To My Beloved
by Abu Maryam Gous

Our separation is heart wrenching, how I long to hold you in my arms again.
To hear the sweetness from you I am longing. The more we are distant the more
the heart aches.

We used to be close albeit for a month...
A time will come again when everyone will be giving you the same attention.
I feel remorse at neglecting you, yet I still resort to it.

Distancing myself from you is not my desire yet I am distant.
Searching for solitude whilst you hold all the solutions
in you, I find comfort and reassurance.

May we be reunited, and strive together, stronger than ever.
Oh my beloved Quran
A little closer we hope to become, day by day, consistently growing not through
haste, for hastiness is what comes from my enemy, the accursed.

My tender heart you enrich through the knowledge I gain,
and so my faith blossoms from your rays, my limbs are yet to obey.
One Day, I hope you will vouch for me, rather than give evidence against me.

Identity
by Abu Maryam Gous

Born with a name as an identity
trying to be accepted in society
pretending to be somebody
to be better eternally
Trudging through adversity is a travesty public opinion swayed
by mediocracy
Traverse the earth with pride and arrogance believing to be better
than everybody
Yet you started as drops of fluid ending up as food of others
Staring in the face of oppression....
the unsightly expression....
tainted realisation of an utterance of the subconscious....
To remain upon the path of salvation....
causal division those in the distance....
looking from a far, what they seem, arn't what they are.....
on this journey what will you carry

Abu Maryam G
by Abu Maryam Gous

Dissemination of information
is powerful
creating an opportunity for
the mind and limbs to formalisation
the lethal weapon being the mind as a nation.

Triggered by the heart filled with love and compassion
A disdained and tainted heart
emits fumes to the mind as a pollution.
Lyrical Jesse James, that ain't me;
just Abu Maryam G.

Shade of Light
by Abu Maryam Gous

Dormant under the shade of light
Crying out in plain sight
Ambushed in the fright of the night
Dwelling in the dark from the blasts of the past
Engulfed while the past still trails in pursuit
hot on the heels....give it an elbow
To break on through to the other side
Let in the light to glide through the future
Taking the steps yet little do we know
what is in store? not to know will suffice
for the calmness to restore.

Until You Come
by Libby Pentreath

I thought I'd come back, thought I'd follow all my words and letters
I thought you'd meet me where we said and
I'd throw my arms around your head
And hold you for an hour – it would hurt to let you go
But I didn't come back did I mum?
And you will never know
You will never see my son grow up, the one I may have had
You'll imagine every day how his hair, his eyes, his smile may be
What games he'd like to play
He and I will live in a special place, a corner behind your eyes
I know you will always sleep and dream and you will care
that I had to go and take my part in the filth and the mud and grime
and that other men as well as me would go before their time...
We'll wait for you, we'll strew the way with those you've loved and lost
Bravado was what we each held
In hands too young and smooth and plump
They made a jarring, aching grasp at life
A cost too much for much too little
So many broken, so many dear hearts cracked
And tears...oh tears, flowing, tidal, wave on wave
And people living on and carrying the memory of the rest of us
..until we meet
I thought I'd come back....but I didn't Mum and I just go on and on and
on
Fighting through the years
To wait until you come Mum
To wait until you come

Remembrance Day 2020
by Libby Pentreath

I went before you - I didn't choose
I got tangled in a game of win and lose
So many of us crumpled and died
As did so many from the other side
We are one world, surely we must see
Please don't let so many follow me
It's not a game, though war still thrives
And each day people lose their lives
Today and every day, be kind
Let's leave the fighting far behind
I will watch over and though I am gone
I give the world a different song
To sing together, live in peace
So fighting, death and injury cease
Remember me this day and all…
And I pray that no more loved ones fall

April 16th 2020

by Libby Pentreath

I cannot buy into the hate that I hear, I read and I see
And neither should any of you
I see vicious words and witch hunt attacks
This is not what we would normally do

It's a frightening time and the news doesn't help
The negatives, numbers and blame
The reasoning doesn't make sense anymore
When so many, young and old are in pain

There should be a light that we view through the dark
And caring and love on all sides
Instead of furrowing brows and withering looks
As we shop, then scuttle home to hide

Do not trust a soul, don't believe in the hype
And those sporting a smile could turn bad
This evil pandemic has troubled our hearts
And turned good into ugly and sad

I have to protect and preserve my belief
That all will be well in the end
That this illness will sink to the bowels of the earth
And we can reconnect and become human again

I know there is empathy and true love out there
But the negatives seem to override
Judgemental and 'holier than thou' attitudes
Tend to play God, overrule and divide

Switch off the relentless updates and falsehoods
The 'I know this', 'it's true' and 'so clear'
Nothing has readied us for something like this
The anxiety, depression and fear

So I will not buy into the hate or the damning
But I do pray one day we will see
That the world has to change and our tunnel sight clear
So that you and I and the whole world can just 'be'

Can be kind in our words and our actions
Can be holding of those that need care
Can smile, give and hug and show empathy and
Always be level and balanced and fair.

Social Work
by Libby Pentreath

Social work is a twisted road
You start off with enthusiasm, the desire to help, a map,knowledge and confidence
You think you can ensure that each journey in each individual case is unique
Everything is able to be sorted...
But no, the uniqueness fades as the challenges grow – it's just some
families have many more that just one difficulty
The difficulties are in layers...you peel one away to discover another
You mend that crack and scream for help as you slip into an even bigger crevice
You climb out to a darkened wall of wrong doing and in the midst of this
And climbing that wall alongside you - are children
Innocent for a few years, then dragged into the family culture and ways
Until you are drained and they are lost. A living fail, a lifelong cost.
Supervision is afforded you, however supervision may not mend the broken
you who has to go back into that home and try to be heard....
You are looked on as a pariah, an intruder, someone who has to be tolerated,
and their visits endured – damned if you do, damned if you don't
You can see through the lies and the enforced good behaviour on any visit...
However, can you sleep at night? No
Can you stop visiting? No
Can you believe that things have changed? Never
Sometimes they do...oft times they don't.
I always believed people could change, and mend potholes in their paths
and learn to walk again
learn to respect and not to lie, learn to care and not to hide their crocodile tears
and the fabricated pain that claws at some form of financial gain
social work is a twisted road, you start standing
and you crumble carrying that daily load.

Wild Wind Batters
by Libby Pentreath

Wild wind batters – wave after wave shatters
The steadfast stony granite clatters
Coastline torn like a well loved coat...to ribbons –
unravelling and lying in sad jagged tatters
Storms, angry in screaming defiance –
Dark clouds, cold rain, grey tides in furious alliance play games
'grab the granite,' - 'toss the stones,'- 'rip up the railings' – 'flood the homes'
The foolhardy standing too close
They view – take photo's, play chicken – was one of them you?
The sea, over so many days, weeping and seeking in so many ways -
freedom while screaming through its foamy haze
screaming as if it's very soul was crazed – and then.......calm -Itstopped.
People ventured to the waterline, like zombies....shocked at what they saw
Silently walking moved to the core
Prom, walkways, jubilee pool – bleeding, broken, bruised and raw.
The ocean retreats - white horses lie down, tides crawl back and behave as predicted
The blue, grey, green and silver surf is reined in
and is soothing, rhythmically musical again.
Social media sites relay the pain the ocean was in
And its desperate attempts to win back and claim more and a deeper wider coastline.
Wild wind battered   Wave upon wave shattered
And we learned firsthand that the steadfast stony granite barrier
wasn't enough to keep sea and land apart
there will always be a rift between ocean and earth
they do not live in complacent consistency – we should always expect the unexpected
in a water fight – the ocean will be a harsh but beautiful victor....

Today
by Libby Pentreath

She summons up some energy
And walks into the room
He's sitting in the darkness
No light dispels the gloom
The atmosphere is tangible
It's calm before the storm
'where do you think you've been?'
He says, 'back to your usual form?'
She tries to quell her shaking
but she can't, she knows full well
though she's learned to read most warning signs
there's some she'll never tell
then – his even toned delivery
of names and labels she must be...
all because the traffic snarled at her
and she was late to make his tea.
She tries backing to the kitchen
put the bags down, get a grip
busy yourself about the room
she told herself - don't flip
don't irritate, don't anger
don't comment, just don't speak
or the bruising you'll be in for
will keep you hiding for a week
...so, she puts away the shopping
Makes the meal, vows she won't stay
But for the sake of peace and sanity
Today is not the day.

The Special Place
by Libby Pentreath

I need to talk about a place, just up the road from me
Where little people gather, they are people we don't see
There is a playground just for them
With a swing, a slide and lights
So they can have fun and games together
Especially at night
When all the children are at home
And safely in their rooms
The garden comes alive in the dark, under the stars and moon
In Mary's faerie garden is a meeting place for all
When faeries, gnomes and elves climb up on Mary's wall
They scamper in the foliage and play on all the toys
They leave their footprints on a stone
To delight the girls and boys
The faeries gather when it's dusk,
 butterflies and grasshoppers come
the magic garden comes to life now the human day is done
because Mary's faerie garden is the place they love to stay
Mary's Faerie garden is the place where faeries play

I Want To Change Myself
by Libby Pentreath

I want to change myself
and the way that I live
instead of taking for me -
I want to learn how to give.
If I can help on my way
I will not ignore
the person crying in a shop or hunched on the shop doorway floor -
Instead of tutting, raising eyes
and screaming at the screen
I will get out, share my pay
buy a coffee - give it away.
Learn to be selfless, learn to share
learn that there are those out there,
on my doorstep, across the world
who need my help - I know it -
Wars are raging, children curled
in life, in death, in pain, despair
dying of hunger, no water or care.
Lives that will end without a beginning
due to our greed, grasping land and wasting of living.
So I am going to change myself
in the years that I have left
and try and help wherever I can,
supporting those bereft.
My shoulders, wide to carry.
My ears, ready for any story.
My heart and mind are open.
I do not need thanks or glory
I just want to change myself
throw false judgements in the bin
turn my hand to help and deal
not turn my nose up or turn on my heel.
Thank the lord, my life is good
I am lucky I have food.
I am lucky I can breathe.
I can only watch and grieve,
I can only pray and hope that the young will lead the way
and grab what's left of living -
make the best of each new day

cont.

I want to change myself.
I want to understand.
I don't have too much time left
but I will still hold love in my hand
and people in my heart
and the hope that we all change
because each day brings its own round
of challenges I've found..
But we can do it, we can move
Rearrange, rethink,
realign and slow down what we don't want to make extinct....

I Didn't Know How It Would Be
by Libby Pentreath

I didn't know how it would be
when you got introduced to me.
Seems a fuzzy memory in my mind-
I look at you now years have passed
a half life over so damn fast.
Never was I prepared for how we change,
how love gets replaced
and it fades into a space
God it seems such a waste
of all the time when we built what we had, now it's turning so bad.
But it's me that is crumpled
you don't even know
that I want to go -
to leave - do my own thing,
have time to explore what my Mum had me for..
Be the person my Dad
always was 'til his end,
be a lover, a shoulder, a rock and a friend -
But not in here - not in now - not until our lives should end.
Hear me shout, let me out
lift me...throw me to myself
let me catch me....let me hatch again
be a baby, shed a shell
I will be vulnerable to viruses,
to being stoned with lies
and I know I will hear your cries as you try to haul me back
to the comfort of noisy storms
as you try as well to hold my heart with arms too hesitant and thin
No more strength and yet you find it -
Somewhere, where? Within?
Without...
Somehow even as you fade and today gets mixed with those bygone
moments,
you keep me, needy, reaching out - how do those threads break anyway?
I could snap each one and run
but no - Because you have nowhere else to go

My Soul Connect
by Paul Phillips

Thank you for being who you are,
Your composure I so dearly admire.

In your presence I sense such calm,
When connected I feel no qualm.

Stillness in time I appear to experience,
Yet, it feels so ecstatically delirious.

The rain has yet to frustrate our mind's meetings,
Loving kindness we show as two true human beings.

We are so different in so many ways,
Our similarities are but stronger, worthy of praise.

Can our souls connect deeper I wonder?
Shaky I get when I look further inside and under.

Writing about you is all that I can do,
Telling you, would only leave us needing to renew.

At your perfect lips I tell myself: 'do not look!'
It's the way I keep my feelings from being unhook.

On your eyes, I rarely fix my gaze,
I am just so happy to be internally ablaze.

Just like you, I too live in a different world,
When we're apart my emotions are left swirled.

The Fragile Soul
by Abul Hussain

By God's will you have left us
To enter a place of eternal bliss
We think about the memories
That remains in our hearts
Sadness we feel when it departs

Your life was surrounded by struggles
We were powerless to help you
Resilience was how you dealt with things
We watched and admired your courage
Feeling proud to be part of your lineage.

Authentic and brave you were with us
Impossible was it to deceive you
Even at old age you were capacious
Wanting to be part of family affairs
Rejoicing as we overcame our impairs.

Prayer and fasting was your conviction
The *tasbeeh* bears your fingerprints
Your pursuit to please your Lord was stark
We envied your devotion and spirituality
Only hoping one day we reach your reality.

Giving charity was your lifelong passion
Despite having little, you gave away a lot
People appreciated you and loved you
Obsession you had to be service to others
Enjoying now the tranquillity it offers.

The Shower
by Suzette Reed

Pitter patter raindrops,
Falling on the ground,
It's caught me out again,
I saw the dark cloud,
I should have brought my raincoat,
But how was I to know,
I thought it was a dry day,
And now the water flows,
My shoes are squishy squashy,
As I walk along,
They weigh my feet down with the wet,
I wanna get home before too long,
So I carry on walking,
In my squishy squashy shoes,
At times like this I always get the shower blues.

The Ice Cream Fairies of Dairyland
by Suzette Reed

In a land far from here lives the Ice cream fairies of Dairyland,
there's Mandy Mint, Sarah Strewberry, Nancy Neopolitan and
Vanessa Vanilla,
they live in their ice cream castles,
their world is cold,
they must not melt,
for they would surely be gone,
they make ice cream for people to eat,
it all would melt if there was heat,
they flitter here and flitter there,
pretty dresses they do wear.
Mandy Mint is dressed in green,
Sarah Strewberry is in pink and is so pretty to be seen,
Nancy Neopolitan wears a multicoloured dress,
And Vanessa Vanilla is in cream as guessed.

The Flower Moon
by Suzette Reed

They call it the flower moon,
it appears in the sky in May,
it shines silvery at night,
and don't appear in the day,
it gives out a lovely glow,
when you watch the water flow,
across the sea,
it reflects back to me,
as it lights up all over the world,
the flower moon,
will be gone by June,
so capture it very soon.

The Naked Tree
by Suzette Reed

There is a tree,
that's near to me,
that doesn't bloom till late,
the other trees are full of leaves,
and blows freely in the breeze
Why isn't that tree blooming yet?
People say,
it will bloom I tell them,
it does it its own way,
it is bare now but wait and see,
the next time you're this way,
it will be full of leaves again,
please listen to what I say.

The Silvery Glow
by Suzette Reed

The moon shines,
it casts shadows,
a silvery Glow across my room,
my cats shadow shows up bright,
on this a calm and silvery night,
the frost glistens upon the ground,
it's so quiet,
there is no sound,
the air is cold,
your breath unfolds,
in curls through the air,
it's too cold to go out,
so I will just stay in,
warm and cosy tonight,
the moon shines on,
throughout the night,
the silver Glow is bright.
31.1.21

The Rainbow
by Suzette Reed

The rainbow bends across the sky,
in shades of colours way up high.
Telling us that rains to come,
before long it comes,
the rain is heavy and quick,
the sky is clouded thick,
where's the sun gone now.
It hides behind the big black clouds
waiting for the rain to pass,
everything is greener,
especially the grass.
21.2.21

Days' Passing
by Amitrajit Raajan

A wave can stir a
mind into a tumultuous tsunami
with An impetus for days'
passing and thinking that love
is a pure energy state
where there is no
lockdown for how a heart
pulses and where there is
no shutdown for how certain
eyes meet like it is
perpetuity for all to contain
and keep it to hurry
it without diminishing it

I Have Nothing To Say
by Amitrajit Raajan

I	have	nothing to	say
Yesterday	you	were	sixty-
one	Presents	are	late
I	went	to	Cormack's
down	Warland	to	buy
monkfish	aubergine	and	chard
I	did	not	put
much	salt	in	and
I	completely	forgot	the
garlic			
Even	so	you	felt
inclined	to	compliment	me
on	my	cooking	thanks

In Memoriam Of Jenny.

by John Cynddylan

Sadly then the Pink Moon's seas did swell.
Unknowing, I heard not its soft Death Knell.
For eight whole months had passed in seeking her
but granite streets did not her story tell.

But, then, a chance reunion did relate
the awful news that told me of her fate.
Full eight months gone she passed
because her heart no more could cope in poorly state.

Oe'rcome with grief do I regret her death
and wish that I could also my last breath
inhale and, with her, sink into th'Eternal Sea
where did I promise her together we would be
sans motion, sans feeling and sans end.

29/04/2021

She
by John Cynddylan

In her eyes I saw trepidation,
something I could not bear to see.
I had rather witness detestation
than a loved one in fear of me.
I but fought to guard her honour
keeping step with my constancy.
What emerged has been of horror,
making Truth her enemy.
Now I see her in the evening
walking on the other side,
knowing well she is not seeing
that Compassion is my guide.
In my daily prayers she figures
yet no more candles do I light.
Scornful am I of the rigours
from those whispering fools of spite.
Weary of those lie-purveyors
ennui, too, is wearing so
'I dismiss those fool gain-sayers
as so much dross the winds do blow.
In sadness now I grieve my love.
Find no Compassion for my grief
nor any solace from above.
For those who hate, hate is their shameful brief.

The Ocean
by John Cynddylan

In the Ocean am I found
where Leviathans abound
and welcome do they find
from me.
But, way above,
where sea meets sky,
doth she maintain
her frothy reign.
Sadness is that knowledge old
that never shall I be so bold
that, at her side, my being should be.
I am The Ocean, she the wave
that breaketh and doth froth
as lightning 'pon my cheek.
And yet do I sustain the myriad cuts
her allies make with their untruths
to punish me.
I am no harm and, yet, am calm
when dumb do they pretend to be.
But Time now singeth out his
terms that we, ere long, consumed
by worms shall be.
A babby's time within the womb is
all we now possess and every
moment gone doth make our
lives much less.
But, should the Froth relent The
Ocean would, as if from Heav'n sent,
believe it all to be, and happy
would he sink to his Infinity.
At last that gentle face within his
sight to such great delight
would win his soul that
gently would he then descend
to rise no more -sans motion
sans feeling-and sans end.

Simon's Silhouette
by John Cynddylan

When the Sun shines so do I
and my thoughts to her do fly.
Will she like this image, too,
of our canine boy, anew?
Boxer dog renown for beauty,
guard for her, that was his duty.
Now they share Eternal Rest
and, to please her, do I test
my skills at sending that pet's
form as silhouettes.
Pure love had he for his dear owner
no other love, he was a loner.
Dear Simon, he gave her his heart,
but came the day, they had to part
and silently he went to rest
beside her bed at my behest.
He suffered less than, if alive,
his life a complex to connive
at being whole as was before
but lacking continence of yore.
Poor Simon, now he lives
in every Sunbeam that I give
to her in fleeting sets
of silhouettes.

Aye
by John Cynddylan

Would I lay with thee in a field of stone?
Would I love thee for thyself alone?
Would I cherish what thou mean'st to me?
Would I then die to be near to thee?
"Aye" is the answer and "aye" 'twill be
and "aye" it rests for Eternity.

And now THE SONG WITH slightly different words and to the tune of The
Summons aka Kelvingrove but sung slowly, like a love song.

Erin, my love.

Would I lay with thee, together, in a field of stone?
Would I love thee then, forever, for thyself alone?
Would I cherish all thou art?
Would I sacrifice my heart?
Would I wait for thee in Heaven
'till you came to me?

Shall we, hand in hand together, fall in love so deep
that our love amongst the heather makes the angels weep?
Will our childrens' children care
of the blows we had to bear
so that they might breathe the air
in our dear land so free?.

Because of you
by Rashma Mehta

Because of you
Because of you I know I excel.
Because of you I know I never struggle as much as I did.
Because of you I know I am worth the risk.
Because of you I stay on the straight and narrow.
Because of you I am stronger than ever before.
Because of you I am braver than ever before.
Because of you I am who I wanna be
Because of you I let out the true me.
Because of you I let out the real me.
Because of you I don't have to pretend.
Because of you i don't feel drained anymore.
Because of you I face my demons without being drawn in.
Because of you I look at myself and think I am more than I thought I could be.
Because of you I don't have to hide anymore.
Because of you I feel wanted.
Because of you I feel valued.
Because of you I know I can achieve what I have always wanted.
Because of you I know I am good enough for the people around me.
Because of you I know I have a flood of people around me.
Because of you I know I have a purpose.
Because of you I see the people who I have and who I don't.
Because of you I found myself.
Because of you I don't feel ashamed to put myself out there for the world to see
my talent just like you did.
Because of you I have a different way of being.
Because of you I look at my life difficultly.
Because of you I am the person I am.
Because of you I got this far.
Because of you I believe in myself.
Because of you I have hope.
Because of you I have strength.
Because of you I have confidence

You Stand Up For Me
by Rashma Mehta

You stand up for me when I can't fight for myself.
You stand up for me when I feel my fears are frightening me to no end.
You stand up for me when I feel so fragile.
You stand up for me when I feel pain.
You stand up for me when I feel abandoned.
You stand up for me when I need you the most.
You stand up for me when I feel broken.
You stand up for me when I get dragged down.
You stand up for me when I am struggling.
You stand up for me when I feel like I'm in a dark place.
You stand up for me when I feel low.
You stand up for me when I don't feel brave enough.
You stand up for me when I don't feel good enough.
You stand up for me when I feel lost.
You stand up for me when I don't have the strength.
You stand up for me when I feel let down.
You stand up for me when I don't feel strong enough.
You stand up for me when I feel I'm in a never ending nightmare.
You stand up for me when I feel like I'm in a war zone.
You stand up for me when I feel lost for words.
You stand up for me when I feel like all I wanna do is cry.
You stand up for me when I feel like all I wanna do is escape my reality.
You stand up for me when all I feel is unnoticed by everyone around me but you.
You stand up for me when I feel invisible.
You stand up for me when I couldn't find my voice.
You stand up for me when I feel no one around me cared but you.
You stand up for me when I felt like I had nothing to give.
You stand up for me when I felt like I was no good.
You stand up for me when I felt like I am not worthy.
You stand up for me when I felt like I was not valued.
You stand up for me when I try and face anything and everything that comes my way.
You stand up for me when I feel no one understands me but you.
You stand up for me when I feel I am alone to show me I am not.
You stand up for me when I feel like all I wanna do is crumble.
You stand up for me when I felt like I was damaged as you show me, I'm not.
You stand up for me when others around me put me down.

You Alwayz Told Me
by Rashma Mehta

You alwayz told me to keep my head held high during my fragile times.
You alwayz told me to keep my head held high during my dark times.
You alwayz told me to keep my head held high during the difficult times that lie ahead for me.
You alwayz told me to keep my head held high during my struggling times I endured.
You alwayz told me to keep my head held high during the hard times I endured.
You alwayz told me to keep my head held high during my rough days.
You alwayz told me to keep my head held high during the pain I endured.
You alwayz told me to keep my head held high when no one else other then you understands me.
You alwayz told me to keep my head held high when all I wanted to do was scream.
You alwayz told me to keep my head held high when all I wanted to do was hide away.
You alwayz told me to keep my head held high when I all I wanted to do was cry
You alwayz told me to keep my head held high when all I thought I would never get to where I am today.
You alwayz told me to keep my head held high and I will get all I want from life.

Looking In The Mirror
by Rashma Mehta

When my fragile past is a reminder of who I was as I look in the mirror.
Looking in the mirror is never knowing what you're going to find.
Looking in the mirror is never knowing how you are going to feel emotionally.
Looking in the mirror is never knowing how the world you're in got so cruel.

Looking in the mirror is not knowing what you're evaluating within yourself.
Looking in the mirror is allowing you to realize who is there for you & who is not.
Looking in the mirror is making you realize who is true to you & who is not.
Looking in the mirror is knowing who will stick by you through thick & thin.

Looking in the mirror will allow you to witness who will stand by you no matter what.
Looking in the mirror is knowing that the people in your life will always look out for you.
Looking in the mirror will determine who will stick around for you.
Looking in the mirror is knowing you have a flood of people around you that will never leave your side throughout the good & bad experiences.

Looking in the mirror lets you figure out who to trust & who not to trust.
Looking in the mirror is knowing that the people around you will take you as you are and not expect you to be someone you're not.
Looking in the mirror is knowing that the people you have in your life will never run a mile.
Looking in the mirror is knowing that the scars & bruises on you don't define you or rule what those around you think about you.
Looking in the mirror is knowing that people around you will take you for the real you and not expect you to be someone who is not original and unique
Looking in the mirror is knowing that the scars, burns, bruises, battles & pain you face explains that whatever you went through you survived and the journey you're on continues.

Echoes
by Rashma Mehta

When my fragile past echoes through the doors.
When my lifelong fears that terrorise me to no end echoes through my mind.
When I try and break my lifelong issues that affect me it echoes like a reminding
sound.
When I don't feel good enough it echoes through me that it truly hurts to be me.

When things get on top of me it echoes to the point I run.
When I feel low it voices echoes as it tells me what to think.
When I feel like a nobody it echoes loudly but you remind me, I am somebody.
When I don't feel brave enough it echoes through to the other side.

When I don't feel strong enough it echoes through the walls.
When I feel like I'm struggling it echoes through me the words you say and I
believe I won't be this way for long.
When I feel like a burden it echoes far out and you catch it to release it.
When hateful or hurtful words come firing at me it echoes through me, I am not
that person.

Never Question
by Rashma Mehta

Never question your fragile past as your past is only a reminder.
Never question how you reach your dreams in your own unique way.
Never question the way your life runs as life itself takes you on a journey of a
lifetime.
Never question the value of yourself.

Never question how strong you can be.
Never question how brave you are.
Never question your abilities and capabilities within yourself.
Never question the outcome of your life as it will lead you down the right path in
the end.

Never question the battles you face as they show how far you have come to get
where you are.
Never question that someone no matter where they are will always be there to give
you the hope, strength and courage you need.
Never question the determination you have to focus on the good things that come
your way.

My Brain
by Jeremy James Lovelady

How's the homeless
Why's my brain
Where's my coat
Eye am sain
Weather summary
Weather or not
Say know to ball games
Now a footballers hot.

DJ
by Jeremy James Lovelady

DJ Sweety Rapper
MC2
Call yourself this
If you dared
Rapping Paper
Christmas no1
Will someone please
Get this rap done.

Will Lives
by Mayar Akash

"when we find love in ourselves,
that is where our 'will' lives,
others call it god.
When you love yourself,
you enumerate 'will' (God),
tis then you are worthy to love outwardly,
 till then - one is unable to love –
simply because of neglect at source;
so eradicate neglect and
then reflect the 'will' that is in you,
tis then when 'will' radiates from you,
tis as the sun's rays kiss off to
that which seeks it."

My Way
by Mayar Akash

If I love you my way
I'll never leave you for a day
and the thing is, don't know it
but it's turning out the way we want it
so while I'm on my way
I want you to remember how much
I love you
I love you
I love you

Oh by the way
I don't even know your name
till then I await.

If I have my way girl
I would never leave you for a second
and the thing is, don't know it
but it's turning out the way favoured
So while I'm on my way
reaching to you
sighing to approve
I want you to know this much
I love you
I love you
I love you my way.

Dear Life
by Mayar Akash

Why is it so painful,
all hurt and aches,
happiness never comes
yet illusions of happiness
always around.

I didn't

Over ten years of longing,
anticipating,
wishing,
praying,
desiring,
dreaming,
wondering,
aching,
hurting,
silently crying,
counting,

You come.

I stumble across you again
2nd time around.

And we met

From the plains of emptiness to an oasis

I can't help myself,
I'm weak and helpless
my mind is defenceless
I'm trying to hold on to myself for myself
for my saneness,
hanging on from
falling into despair.

I Made My Life
by Mayar Akash

I made my life so that you can:
grow off it
learn off it
educate off it
be off it
secure your future with it

Whatever you wanted off it

in return for little bit of understanding and love

my life bears witness to your sacrifices
my life accepts responsibility for your kindness
my life lives your pain and sadness
my life's destiny was to caress and take away that

give you all that will flourish you and make you happy
if you become happy I will be happy

all that I needed from you was time
to allow what I've started to give.

Roll Call

We at Penny Authors like to recognise, remind and remember all the Penny Authors that have taken part past always and present:

1. Mayar Akash (Founder)
2. Zainab Khan,
3. Paul Harvey,
4. Isaac Harvey,
5. Rebekah Vaughan,
6. Rabia Mehmood,
7. Tamanna Parveen,
8. Ellis Dixon-King,
9. Liam Newton,
10. Professor Muhammad Nurul Huque,
11. Kalam Choudhury,
12. Rashma Mehta,
13. Mathew Saunders Whiting
14. Akik Miah
15. NirmalKaur
16. Mayar Akash
17. Julie Archbold
18. Lora Ashman
19. John Robert Gordon
20. Julie Anne Wheeler
21. Late Joan Hodge
22. Ruth Lewarne
23. Bhupendra M. Gandhi
24. Nicki & Laura Ellis
25. Alga Statham
26. Jeremy J. Lovelady (Artist & Poet)
27. Peter Fox (Artist)
28. Jamal Hasan
29. Stephen Goldsmith
30. Clare Saunders Whiting
31. Sally Walker
32. Elsa Kiernanfox
33. Jaida Begum
34. Abdul Mannan
35. John Dillon
36. Suzette Reed
37. Sandra Sanjeet Green

38. Coral Dodsworth (Artist)
39. Amitrajit Raajan
40. Chris York
41. Ossian Hughes
42. Stuart Cooper
43. Mustak Ahmed Mustafa
44. Samiul Fox
45. Ayesha Chowdhury
46. Ferdous Rahman
47. Abu Maryam Gous
48. Steve Willoughby
49. Abul Hussain
50. Libby Pentreath
51. Paul Peters
52. Adrian Smith (Artist)

For more information or if you would like to submit your work for inclusion, email: pennyauthers@yahoo.co.uk.

MAPublisher Catalogue

ISBN/Titles /Image/Author	Descriptions
978-1-910499-15-3 Anthology One By Penny Authors	This is the first of the Penny Authors Anthologies. Titled, "Anthology One". It is filled with so many different journeys.
978-1-910499-17-7 Anthology Two By Penny Authors	This is the second of the Penny Authors Anthologies. Titled, "Anthology Two". It is filled with so many more different journeys. Many are the same journeys but experienced by different people of various cultures. It is a wonderful place to expand ones horizon.
978-1-910499-29-0 V3 Book of Lived By Penny Authors	V3 Book of Lived". After the experiences gained from the previous two publications, It became clear that these books were more than average poetry books, These were lived moments recorded. This is the first anthology with the new title.
978-1-910499-35-1 V4 Book of Lived By Penny Authors	After the third instalment the momentum for the Penny Authors to come together and share their life journey in so that the reader finds that "missing Jigsaw" piece in their life. If this anthology serves one soul then it has served its purpose.
978-1-910499-50-4 V5 Book of Lived By Penny Authors	This issue is truly the vision, new poets and even the cover image is by a local artist. Volume 5 is the 1st that is what the founder's purpose for this anthology was - to give aspiring writers and artist a hand.
978-1-9100499-54-2 V6 Book of Lived By Penny Authors	This issue is truly a journey, it encapsulates the Covid 19 Pandemic, the lockdown. Penny Authors stayed connected via email and collectively recorded their experience of the isolation and the threat the disease posed to humans in every corner of the world.

ISBN/Titles /Image/Author	Descriptions
978-1-910499-02-3 (eBook) & 978-1-910499-00-9 (Paperback) Father to child By Mayar Akash	This EBook version Father to Child is a collection of inspirational poems and musings that follow the author's life from his own childhood up to when he had children of his own, and wishes to pass some of wisdom to them.
978-1-910499-16-0 River of Life By Mayar Akash	This journey in the river of life, a metaphor for living, a contrast between the British life and the Bangladeshi lives' in both parts of the world. Reflect on the integrational change acquired and adopted as a result of living in UK.
978-1-910499-14-6 The Halloweeen Poem By Zainab Khan	This short poetry book written by Zainab who was an 8-year-old. She writes about her experience of Halloween in poetry form, especially as a young Bangladeshi Muslim growing up and integrating into the British society.
978-1-910499-36-8 Delirious By Liam Newton	Music is powerful enough to change people's views on aspects of the society they live in or the world around them. In this book the writer gives the reader snapshot insight of his life in the form of lyrics. Music keeps him going and hope it keeps you going too
978-1-910499-39-9 Eyewithin By Mayar Akash	This is the 3rd book of Mayar Akash. The book catalogues the lost paintings by himself.
978-1-910499-37-5 My Dream World By Rashma Mehta	This is the first of Rashma's book filled with her imaginary world of experiences and perception.

978-1-910499-41-2 When You Look Back By Rashma Mehta	This is Rashma's 2nd book filled with her imaginary world of experiences and perception.
978-1-910499-49-8 Cry For Help By Bhupendra M. Gandhi	This is Bhupendra's 1st poetry book published through the Penny Authors' facilities. His work is truly inspirational and has depth that make to fell human.
978-1-910499-42-9 My Life Book 1 By Mayar Akash	This is Mayar's unabridged collection of classics catalogued. Book 1 of his work to 2016.
978-1-910499-44-3 My Life Book 2 By Mayar Akash	This is Mayar's unabridged collection of classics catalogued. Book 2 of his work to 2016.
978-1-910499-53-5 Angel Eyez By Rashma Mehta	This is Rashma's next accomplishment over 400 hundred pages of her creative writing following on from her previous two books.
9781910499-69-6 Consciousness Mustak A Mustafa	The writer highlighted some of the events that have been taken place in his life. Some of the fantasies have been painted in an art form and some of his writing has demonstrated the rhythm of song in his poems.

For more information you can email: pennyauthors@yahoo.co.uk. All books are available on-line store.